The Misfits

Based on the television series created by Josh Schwartz including the episode 'The Heights', written by Debra J. Fisher & Erica Messer; the episode 'The Perfect Couple', written by Allan Heinberg; the episode 'The Homecoming', written by Josh Schwartz and Bryan Oh; and the episode 'The Best Chrismukkah Ever', written by Stephanie Savage

Adapted by: Penny Hancock
Commissioning Editor: Jacquie Bloese
Editor: Fiona Davis
Designer: Dawn Wilson
Picture research: Emma Bree
Photo credits:
Cover and inside images courtesy of Warner Bros.
Cover: J. Frechet/Alamy.
Page 60: Image 100.
Page 61: Imagesource/Rex Features; Imagesource.

Copyright © 2007 Warner Bros. Entertainment Inc.
THE O.C. and all related characters and elements are trademarks of and © Warner Bros. Entertainment Inc.
WB SHIELD: ™ & © Warner Bros. Entertainment Inc.
MARY 6707

Fact File text and design © Scholastic Ltd. 2007
All rights reserved.

Published by Scholastic Ltd.

No part of this publication may be reproduced in whole or in part, or stored in a retrieval system, or transmitted in any form or by any means, electronic, mechanical, photocopying, recording or otherwise, without written permission of the publisher. For information regarding permission write to:

Mary Glasgow Magazines (Scholastic Ltd.)
Euston House
24 Eversholt Street
London NW1 1DB

Printed in Singapore. Reprinted in 2009.
This edition printed in 2011.

Contents	Page
The Misfits	**4–55**
People and places	**4–5**
The story so far	**6**
Chapter 1: The misfits	**7**
Chapter 2: The truth	**14**
Chapter 3: Carnival	**19**
Chapter 4: A family again?	**23**
Chapter 5: The perfect couple	**27**
Chapter 6: A call for help	**33**
Chapter 7: Thanksgiving	**38**
Chapter 8: Christmas shopping	**43**
Chapter 9: Chrismukkah	**48**
Fact Files	**56–61**
The coolest job in the world?	56
Adam Brody	58
Under age? What the law says …	60
Self-Study Activities	**62–64**
New Words!	inside back cover

PEOPLE AND PLACES

SANDY COHEN
Seth's dad.

JULIE & JIMMY COOPER
Marissa's parents.

LUKE WARD
He's been Marissa's boyfriend for six years, but since Ryan arrived, there have been big problems …

ANNA STERN
She's just arrived from Pittsburg and she's a bit different. She likes Seth, but Seth has always liked Summer …

SETH COHEN
He used to be the Newport geek – but things have changed since Ryan got here. This year could be interesting …

MARISSA COOPER
She seems to have everything but life is still difficult. Her mom and dad are getting divorced. And now she's broken up with her boyfriend, Luke. But drinking helps her forget her problems …

THE N

4

RYAN ATWOOD
He's from Chino and he's been having a hard time. Now he's living with the Cohens and he wants things to change. He likes Marissa – and she likes him – but they're from different worlds …

KIRSTEN COHEN & CALEB NICHOL
Seth's mom and grandfather.

SUMMER ROBERTS
She's Marissa's best friend and she's usually only seen with the coolest guys. So why is she starting to have feelings for Seth Cohen?

PLACES
Newport Beach, Orange County Home to the the rich and the beautiful …
Chino, San Bernandino County Chino is only an hour's drive from Newport Beach, but it's a different kind of California …
Harbor School The best school in Newport Beach.

The story so far

Marissa's diary

I don't know what I'm going to do ... I hate being in this hospital. I want to go home. But I don't know where 'home' is. I don't want to live with Mom. Maybe I could stay at Dad's ...

Mom thinks I'm crazy and I should go to a special hospital. I'm not crazy — she just doesn't know what to do with me. She says everything was OK before Ryan got here. She hates him, but it's only because he's from Chino and he's poor. Money is so important to her.

Ryan came to see me the other day. He's cool and I know he understands. He knows the Mexico thing was just a stupid mistake.

When we left for Tijuana, I was OK. Summer asked me to go with her. Seth and Ryan came too. I thought it would be fun. But then Dad called to say that he and Mom were getting divorced. In Tijuana we went to a bar and Luke was there too. I saw him kissing another girl. I couldn't believe it.

I started drinking. I just wanted to forget everything. And I took some pills. I don't remember anything after that. When the others found me, they thought I might die.

Ryan makes me feel better. I hope he comes to see me again soon. He's had a hard time too. His brother's in prison because he stole a car. Ryan was with him and he had to go to Juvie*. His mom left him and now he's living with the Cohens. He wants a new start, like me. I really hope we can be friends.

I'd better go. The doctor's here now ...

* Juvie is a prison for young (juvenile) criminals.

CHAPTER 1
The misfits

'This year is going to be different ... better ...' said Seth. 'It even smells different. Can you smell it?'

Ryan didn't say anything. The two friends were walking across the beautiful, green gardens of Harbor School. It was Ryan's first day. It hadn't been easy to get a place here and Ryan felt a bit nervous. Would he fit in? But Seth went on talking happily.

'Before, I always used to sit on my own. I had lunch on my own. I studied on my own. But this year you're here. When people see me with you, they'll think I'm cool!'

Just then, a big water polo player walked by and pushed Seth hard. 'Loser!' he said.

Seth picked up the books that he'd dropped and smiled at Ryan. 'See? That wasn't too bad! Last year was worse than that ...'

Ryan helped Seth get up. He'd promised Sandy and

Kirsten that he would stay out of trouble. It wasn't going to be easy.

***

Best friends Summer and Marissa had just arrived at school. Marissa waited by the car as Summer put on her make-up.

'I don't want to be here,' Marissa was saying to Summer. 'Everyone's talking about what happened to me.'

'Coop*, they don't even know what happened to you!' Summer said.

'If they don't know, they'll find something else to say about me,' said Marissa. 'And that's worse.'

* Marissa's surname is Cooper. Summer calls her 'Coop'.

'Hey,' said Summer slowly. '*I'll* tell you what's worse. It's Seth Cohen.'

Marissa looked up. When she saw Seth and Ryan coming towards them, she felt happier. Ryan always made her feel better.

'Hey, Ryan,' she said. 'What's your first class?'

Ryan pulled out a piece of paper from his pocket and studied it carefully.

'It's Maths ... with Mr Corcetti,' he said finally.

'Good. That's my first class too. Come on, I'll show you where it is.'

'Thanks,' Ryan began to walk with her.

'Hey! Wait for me,' said Seth, but Summer stopped him.

'Don't you get it, Cohen? They want to be alone!' she said.

'Really?' said Seth. 'Well, then I guess I'll walk with you.'

Summer sighed. 'OK. If you have to ...' she said.

Ryan looked quickly at Marissa as he walked along with her. He wanted to hold her hand, but he didn't know how she felt. She had broken up with Luke, but was she ready to be with him? Also, he wasn't sure about the rules here. Did kids hold hands at Harbor School? Perhaps they weren't allowed to. It was so different to his old school in Chino. In Chino, kids were allowed to do almost anything!

'We could go somewhere else,' said Marissa. 'I'd like to get in my car and drive to the beach. Everyone's looking at me, and I don't like it.'

'No, they're not. They're looking at *me*,' said Ryan.

'You didn't try to kill yourself.'

'No, but you didn't spend the summer in Juvie!' said Ryan, and they laughed. OK, so the other kids in Newport all seemed perfect. But Ryan and Marissa's problems were making them feel close.

'So … what do you think? Shall we get in your car and go?' Ryan asked.

'Better not,' sighed Marissa. 'I'd better not get in more trouble.'

'No,' Ryan agreed. 'I've got to be good, too, or they'll ask me to leave.'

'We could do something tonight,' said Marissa. 'I'll come to the pool house and say hi.'

'Great!' said Ryan. And then he took her hand, just for a second.

***

Behind them, Seth was busy making plans for spending the day with Summer. Summer didn't look happy.

'So I was thinking …' he said slowly. 'We could eat lunch together. Sit under the trees.'

'And why would I eat lunch with you?' said Summer. Yes, Seth had been cool in Mexico and he looked quite cute today, but … what was she thinking? This was Seth Cohen!

'I thought we were friends now … after Mexico …' said Seth, feeling a little hurt.

'We're not in Mexico now!' Summer replied.

Before Seth could say anything else, someone called out to him, 'Cohen!'

Seth turned. A small, pretty girl was coming towards them.

'Anna! What are you doing here?' Seth put his arms around her.

'I left Pittsburg!' Anna said.

'So you're coming to Harbor instead? Hey, that's cool!' said Seth. He felt really pleased. 'Summer, do you remember Anna? '

'How could I forget?' Summer said.

Summer looked at Anna's clothes. She looked cool and different, with her long earrings and short blonde hair. Summer didn't like the look of Anna. Perhaps it was because Seth seemed to like her so much.

'Let's go,' she said. 'We're going to be late for class.'

***

Later, in the science class, Summer went over to Seth.

'You're going to work with me, aren't you, Seth?' she said. 'You can do all the boring things – like writing reports.'

'Oh, yes!' he said. 'I'd love to work with you!'

He couldn't believe it! This was the first time Summer had spoken to him before he spoke to her first! It was too good to be true.

But then someone put a hand on his arm. It was Anna.

'Just a minute,' said Anna, looking at Summer. 'Seth promised to work with me.'

'Well … I don't know …' Seth began. Anna was looking at him, trying to say something, but he didn't get it.

Then he looked over at Summer. Summer was looking angrily at Anna. Was it possible that Summer was getting jealous? Seth couldn't believe it.

'Sorry, Summer,' he said. 'I'm working with Anna.'

Summer pretended she didn't care. 'Whatever,' she said and went to work with Jordan Cypher. Jordan Cypher was even less popular than Seth Cohen.

'What's happening?' she wondered. 'Do I have feelings for Seth? But that's crazy – he's such a loser!'

After class, Summer waited for Seth. Maybe they could have lunch together after all. But Seth was talking to Anna. He walked out of the class without even seeing her.

'Cohen!' Summer cried, but Seth didn't hear her either.

   She felt upset. Seth was more interested in Anna than her. And she felt jealous! 'What's wrong with me?' she wondered.
   'You've upset Summer,' Anna said.
   'What?' said Seth and immediately turned back.
   'Don't go back to her!' Anna cried. 'You know what your problem is? You're too nice to her. Girls don't like guys who are always nice. If you really like Summer, stop trying to please her.'

'Hey, you're probably right. You understand these things. You're a girl …' said Seth.

'Thanks for noticing!' said Anna.

Seth didn't see the way Anna looked at him.

'I know! You could give me advice – help me win Summer!' he said, kissing the top of her head. 'Thank you, thank you, thank you! This is going to be great!'

'Yeah – really great,' said Anna to herself angrily, and followed Seth outside.

CHAPTER 2
The truth

That evening, Ryan was sitting in the pool house next to a pile of books. The Cohens had made the pool house as comfortable as possible for him. Things were going well. At last he had his own space. And he was at Harbor School. But the work at Harbor was very difficult. It was much harder than the work at his last school. 'How will I ever catch up?' he thought. 'There are so many books to read!'

There was a knock on the door and he looked up. It was Marissa, looking great as usual.

'Hi,' she said, stopping just inside the door.

'Hey,' Ryan said, 'Were you at your mom's?'

'Yeah, but she wasn't home, thank God. What are you reading?'

'Solzhenitzyn.*'

'Oh yeah, I read that last year. It's sad.'

'I've only read the first chapter. And we have a test on it this Friday.'

'Perhaps you need to go out for an hour?'

'I'd love to go out, but I've got to read some more,' said Ryan. 'If I don't catch up, they won't let me stay at Harbor.'

'Oh ... OK,' said Marissa. She looked sad and Ryan took

* Solzhenitzyn is a twentieth-century Russian writer who won the Nobel Prize for Literature in 1970.

her hand.

'Look, Marissa, you know I really want to spend time with you, but …' He waved at the piles of work. 'Maybe we could do something this weekend …'

'I can't. I'm working at the carnival,' said Marissa.

'Carnival?'

'Every year we have a carnival to make money for school.'

'Well … why don't I go with you?' Ryan said.

'Great!' Marissa said, starting to leave. 'Bye, then.'

'See you tomorrow,' Ryan said and picked up his book again.

Ryan felt bad. Marissa had looked so sad. He wanted to run after her. 'This stupid work!' he thought. 'Maybe I'll just forget it.' He picked up his jacket, but then there was another knock on the door. Too late. It was Sandy. He had a cup of coffee for Ryan.

'How are you getting on?' asked Sandy.

'Not good,' said Ryan slowly. 'I find this work really hard.'

'You can do it. You're as clever as any other kid at Harbor.'

Ryan had always wanted to hear words like that. He didn't know his own father very well, but he hoped he was someone like Sandy. He wanted to throw his arms around him, but instead he picked up the cup and looked away.

'Thanks for the coffee,' he said.

***

Marissa sat in her car. She didn't know what to do. Summer was busy. None of her other friends wanted to see her now. And she didn't want to see Luke. She decided to go home. Maybe she could go and see a movie with her dad. She drove back to the apartment, but when she got there, Jimmy was out. He had left a note and some money on the fridge. 'Buy some pizza. See you later.'

'Maybe I should do some school work. Like Ryan,' Marissa thought, but she just looked at the same page in her maths book for half an hour. 'What's wrong with me?' she wondered. 'Lots of kids' parents get divorced. Lots of girls break up with their boyfriends. Why do these problems seem so bad to me? Maybe Mom is right. Maybe I need to talk to a therapist.'

Her thoughts went round and round. She got up and looked at the money her dad had left. She really should eat something. She opened the fridge. There wasn't much to eat, but there *was* a bottle of vodka. She poured herself a large glass and drank it. She couldn't taste it, but she could feel it. And it felt better. Sometimes she put some water in the bottle. Then her dad wouldn't know she'd drunk the vodka. But this time she just poured a second glass. And after that she stopped thinking. Soon she couldn't feel anything at all.

***

'Hey, Marissa, look what I've got for you!' It was the next morning and Jimmy had got her a coffee and her favourite bagels*. Marissa felt terrible and she didn't want to go to school. But she didn't want to explain to Jimmy. Life was hard enough for him already.

'Thanks,' she said, trying to smile.

She finally got to school – late. And she was getting her books out of her bag when things got a lot worse.

'Marissa!' She looked up. It was Luke. She hadn't seen

* A bagel is a type of bread in the shape of a ring.

him since Mexico.

She started to walk away, but Luke stopped her.

'Look, Marissa,' he said. 'I'm really sorry for what happened in Mexico. It was a mistake, a stupid mistake …'

'I don't want to talk about it,' said Marissa. 'You were with another girl. There is nothing more to talk about.'

'But Marissa, I never meant to hurt you. Really,' Luke said. Then, to her surprise, he began to cry.

'Please!' she said. 'Please stop crying. It's OK.'

'It isn't OK,' he said. 'You're my best friend. You always have been. I love you and I don't know what I'm going to do without you.'

Ryan was walking past the classroom when he heard voices. He stopped and looked through the door. He saw Luke and Marissa standing close together and he heard Luke's words. He wanted to run in and hit Luke hard. But since he got to Newport, Ryan had learnt that fighting was not always the answer. Instead, he walked away, and he didn't hear Marissa's reply.

'I'm sorry, Luke,' she said, 'but I can't forget what you did. We're finished.'

***

Ryan was still angry at football practice after school. The only person Ryan could see on the field was Luke. They were playing on different teams. When Luke got the ball, Ryan ran after him. Now he couldn't stop himself. He ran towards Luke and pushed him to the ground.

The teacher ran towards them, shouting. Ryan had really wanted to hurt Luke, but now he felt bad.

He held out his hand to help Luke get up, but Luke didn't move.

'What's the matter with you?' shouted the teacher. 'That was much too hard. Now we've lost our best player.'

***

When Ryan saw Marissa he felt even worse. She was waiting for him outside the school.

'What do you think you were doing?' Marissa asked Ryan angrily. 'You really hurt Luke. I saw you!'

'It was a game. You know all about games, don't you?' said Ryan.

'What do you mean?' asked Marissa, surprised.

'I saw you!' Ryan said. 'I saw you and Luke talking.'

'Are you spying on me?' cried Marissa.

'I wanted to know the truth.'

'Well, now you know,' said Marissa, and she walked away.

Ryan watched her go. He was so angry. But was he angry with Marissa, or was he angry with himself? He didn't know anymore.

CHAPTER 3
Carnival

The carnival was the best charity event of the year. For once, it was fun to help make money for Harbor.

Ryan, Seth and Anna were at the skeeball*.

'Look!' said Seth. 'I'm really good at this.' He threw a ball and missed.

'Watch me!' Anna laughed and won a toy. 'You can keep this …' she said, giving it to Seth, 'and remember me.'

'Don't worry, I'll never forget you!' he said, putting his arm around her.

She moved closer to him, but suddenly he took his arm away – Ryan was smiling at them.

'Have you seen Marissa?' said Ryan. 'I really need to talk to her.'

'She was near the ferris wheel,' said Anna.

'Summer might be there too,' said Seth. 'Come on,

---
* Skeeball is a game which is similar to bowling.

Anna.' He started to go, but Anna didn't move. She looked fed up. 'What?' he asked.

'Nothing,' she said. 'Just come on.' And she ran after Ryan, leaving Seth to follow.

On his way to the ferris wheel, Ryan met Luke.

'Look,' Ryan said quickly, 'I'm sorry about yesterday.'

Luke looked past Ryan – he had seen Marissa waiting to get on the ferris wheel. Ryan saw her too and immediately forgot all about Luke.

'I think I get it,' said Luke as Ryan ran towards Marissa.

Ryan pushed past Summer and climbed into the seat next to Marissa.

'What do you think you're doing?' Marissa asked.

She looked angry with him, but it was too late. The wheel was moving.

'I need to talk to you,' said Ryan. 'Oh God!'

The seat was rising into the air.

'What's wrong?' asked Marissa.

'I'm afraid of heights.'

'Then why did you follow me here?' she asked

'I need to … I wanted to say sorry,' said Ryan.

Suddenly the wheel stopped. They were at the top of the ride. Ryan looked down. It was a long way down. He began to feel sick.

Now that Ryan had said sorry, Marissa didn't mind. She was enjoying sitting there so close to Ryan.

Back on the ground, Anna had a plan. 'Don't start it yet,' she told the ferris wheel operator. 'Leave them up there for a bit longer. They need to talk.'

'So that's Marissa and Ryan,' thought Anna. 'What about me and Seth?'

She looked at Seth. He was watching Marissa and Ryan on the wheel.

'So … Cohen … there's something I want to tell you,' she said.

He turned to look at her. 'What?' he asked.

'This,' said Anna. She reached her arms up around his neck and kissed him.

Seth couldn't believe it. A girl was kissing him! Girls never kissed him. He closed his eyes. He didn't want Anna to move away. He wanted this kiss to go on forever.

But when he opened his eyes, his heart nearly stopped. There, in front of him, was Summer, and she was staring at them.

'This has to be part of Anna's plan,' Seth thought. 'The best plan ever!'

And he watched Summer walking away.

***

Up in the air, Marissa moved closer to Ryan.

'Are you OK?' she asked him.

'I think so,' he said. He was trying not to think about the height.

'Marissa … I need to tell you something. I don't talk a lot, but I can talk to you. And I like you – I really like you.'

'Ryan …' she said, and then she was kissing him, her hands in his hair.

Ryan forgot all about the height. And when the wheel started to move again, he didn't even notice.

CHAPTER 4
A family again?

It was six weeks after the start of term at Harbor, and Ryan still had a lot of catching up to do. But when Marissa was in his arms, he could forget all about it. Ryan had never felt like this before. Yes, he had loved Theresa, the girl who lived next door to him in Chino – but not like this. He knew Theresa would be OK without him. She was strong. With Marissa, he felt different. He wanted to protect her. He didn't want her to be sad again.

Marissa felt the same way about Ryan.

'You really like Ryan, don't you, Coop?' Summer said to Marissa as they walked across the school gardens one day.

'Yeah,' said Marissa, smiling. 'But I want to go slowly. I don't want to hurt him. He's been having a hard time.'

'Don't go too slowly!' said Summer. 'Boys don't like that!'

'Don't worry!' said Marissa 'We're good together. I understand him, and he understands me.'

When she was with Ryan, Marissa stopped thinking about her problems at home. But the problems didn't disappear. That afternoon, she opened the door to her dad's apartment and was shocked to see her mother, Julie, sitting there.

Marissa didn't want to see her mother. She couldn't forget what her mother had said to her in hospital.

'What are *you* doing here?' asked Marissa coldly.

Jimmy came into the room with some cold drinks. He didn't seem angry. 'Your mom has some news for you,' he said.

'I wanted to tell you that I'm having a party …' said Julie.

'No,' said Marissa. She knew what her mother would say next.

'It's to make money for the Children's Hospital,' Julie added. 'I want you to come, Marissa. Please. Your father has already agreed.'

She looked at Jimmy and he smiled.

Marissa felt upset. How could her dad be nice to her mom? How could he forgive her for walking away when he was in trouble?

'We have to forget about what happened with your father's business,' Julie went on. 'I want Newport people to see us – the Coopers – together. I want them to think what a strong family we are.'

Marissa didn't answer.

'Please, Marissa. This is important to me,' said Julie. There were tears in her eyes. 'I'm so sorry for what happened before. But Marissa, I was afraid. Everything was so awful. Your father's business. The things you did in Mexico. But I was wrong. I just want us to be a family again.'

Jimmy smiled and moved closer to Julie. Then Julie took Marissa's hand. Before Marissa could stop herself, she put her arms around her parents.

'Perhaps Mom is right,' she thought. ' Perhaps we can be a family again.' And it felt good.

***

Ryan was lying on his bed in the pool house reading one of Seth's *Fantastic Four* comics. There was a knock at the door. It was Marissa.

'Hey,' he said pulling her down next to him. 'I was just thinking about you. You OK?' he asked.

'Yes, I think so. I saw my mom,' said Marissa. 'She said she was sorry. She wants us to be a family again. And she wants us – you and me – to go to her party.'

'But your mom hates me ...' began Ryan.

'I think she's really changed,' said Marissa. 'You must come.'

'Oh yeah? Why?'

'It's on Seth's grandfather's yacht.'

'Is that the only reason?' said Ryan, laughing.

'And I want you with me,' said Marissa, kissing him. They fell back on his bed.

It felt so good to be together. It was always difficult for Marissa to leave. But it was getting late.

'I've got to go,' she said. 'But I'll see you tomorrow.'

Ryan heard Marissa's car drive away. It was too late now to start school work. He decided to go and find Seth. Outside it was a warm and starry night. He looked up at the stars and, for once, felt truly happy.

Then he heard a car arriving at Julie Cooper's house next door. Julie got out, followed by Seth's grandfather, Caleb. They stood there under the light. They were very close together. Ryan watched as Julie kissed Caleb. They stood kissing for a few minutes.

Shocked, Ryan moved away. Too late. Julie looked up and their eyes met.

Ryan walked quickly back into the Cohens' house. 'Just when things seemed better!' thought Ryan. 'How am I going to tell Marissa?'

CHAPTER 5
The perfect couple

Julie Cooper wanted the party to be special. And it was. Caleb's yacht was covered with bright lights. Ryan stared at the beautiful people in their designer clothes and all the waiters offering expensive drinks.

Seth and Anna, Marissa and Ryan had all arrived together. Anna was wearing an expensive dress. She looked older and beautiful. But when she laughed, you could still see the real Anna in her eyes. Seth couldn't stop looking at her.

Julie and Jimmy Cooper stood at the entrance to the yacht, welcoming the guests. They looked like the perfect couple. Marissa smiled and kissed both of them. When Julie saw Ryan, she took his arm and led him a few steps away from the others.

'This is our chance to start again as a family,' she said quietly.

'Oh yeah?' Ryan replied angrily. 'So what were you doing with Caleb Nichol?'

'You don't know what you're talking about,' said Julie coldly.

'I know that Marissa believes you still love her dad. You're lying to her!'

Ryan walked away, and Julie had to let him go.

***

Marissa and Summer were standing at the bar. They were watching Seth and Anna laughing together on the other side of the yacht.

'What is Seth doing with Anna? I don't like her,' said Summer.

'Anna's cool,' said Marissa. 'Maybe you don't like her because she likes Seth Cohen!'

'*I* don't like Seth Cohen!' said Summer.

'But he likes *you*!' said Marissa. Summer opened her mouth to speak, but Marissa had seen Ryan.

'Come on,' she said to him. 'Let's get a drink.'

Ryan and Marissa walked away together.

'Maybe Marissa's right …' thought Summer.

***

Ryan and Marissa found a quiet part of the yacht.

'I'm so happy for my mom and dad,' Marissa said. 'Now they are back together, maybe I'll be living next door to you again!'

Ryan felt so bad. He didn't want to upset Marissa, but he couldn't keep this secret from her.

'Maybe they're not together again,' he said.

'What do you mean?' Marissa asked quickly.

'Look,' he said, 'I didn't want to tell you this, but I have to. I saw your mom with Caleb Nichol, and they were kissing.'

'What?'

Ryan wanted to hold Marissa. He wanted to tell her everything would be OK. But Marissa was already moving away from him.

'I'm sorry, Marissa.'

Marissa looked at Ryan for a few minutes more, then she walked away. Ryan followed.

***

'This is a strange place,' Anna was saying to Seth. 'People don't look like this in Pittsburg.'

'Like what?'

'Very rich and very thin!'

'So what do you think of Newport?'

'I didn't like it at first,' said Anna. 'I didn't think I'd fit in. But I like it now.' She looked at him as if she was ready to kiss him. Then Seth suddenly realised. Anna liked him. She really liked him. And it would be great to be with her. But what about Summer? He had always liked Summer. Since he could remember. He'd named his boat after her. He'd made a CD mix of songs which had the word 'summer' in them. He couldn't even think of one song with the word 'Anna' in it.

'I'll get some drinks,' he said. He needed some time to think. And before Anna could reply, he started to move towards the bar.

***

Seth was coming back from the bar, when a door opened, and Summer appeared.

'Seth!' she said quietly.

He looked at her, surprised.

She pulled him into a room. And before he could speak, she pushed him against the wall and started kissing him.

'Oh, wow! This must be a dream – I must remember every second!' thought Seth. 'It can't really be happening.'

When Summer stopped kissing him, she looked at him. 'Oh no!' she cried.

'What now?' thought Seth.

'I like Seth Cohen!' said Summer, still not really believing it. And then she ran away.

***

Julie Cooper stood in the middle of the yacht. She was holding a microphone. A crowd of people were watching her.

'Thank you all for coming tonight,' she said. 'We've made two hundred thousand dollars for the Children's Hospital. And now we are giving away a romantic week for two in Hawaii. I'd like to ask my beautiful daughter, Marissa, to read the names of the winners.'

Marissa looked at Ryan. 'Ready for this?'

'Why don't we just go?' he said, but she was already walking towards the microphone. Ryan couldn't look. What was she going to say?

Everyone was watching and listening.

'Let's thank my mother and Caleb Nichol for all their hard work. If anyone should go on a romantic week for two, it's the two of them. Aren't they just the perfect couple?'

The guests had become silent. Julie moved to take the microphone, but Marissa wouldn't let her.

'They've been keeping their romance secret,' she went

on. 'Well, it's not a secret anymore. Congratulations, guys!'

Marissa dropped the microphone as the guests started to talk. Julie stayed where she was, too shocked to move. She could see Jimmy coming towards her. He looked angry.

***

People began to leave the yacht.

'Guess what you missed?' Anna said to Seth. He had come back with drinks, but his head was full of Summer. 'What?' he asked.

'I'll tell you on the way home,' said Anna, putting her arm around him.

Marissa and Ryan also started to leave. Marissa was shaking as Julie Cooper ran up to her.

'What do you think you were doing?' she shouted angrily.

'I was just telling the truth,' said Marissa. 'But you don't know what truth is. You lied to me. You said you wanted us to be a family again.'

'Yes, we can be a family again.'

'What about Dad?'

'I will always love your father,' Julie said calmly. 'But because of what he's done, we have no future together.'

'Then you have no future with me either!' said Marissa. 'Come on, Ryan.' She pulled Ryan's hand and they got into her car.

They drove away and Ryan looked back. There was Julie Cooper, standing alone, as all her guests left. Just for a moment, Ryan felt really sorry for her.

CHAPTER 6
A call for help

Ryan had received his report from Harbor, and the news was not good.

'Maybe I can help,' said Sandy. 'I used to be good at science.'

'I just need a couple of weeks with nothing else to do,' said Ryan. 'Then I can catch up.'

'Well, you have eight days' holiday,' said Kirsten, 'for Thanksgiving.* Why don't you sit at the kitchen table and work for a few hours every day? You'll start to feel more confident.'

So Ryan started on his homework on the first day of the holidays. He got up early in the morning and worked until late at night. And after a couple of days, he was beginning to understand the work better.

***

* Thanksgiving is a North American celebration in November.

On the third day of the holidays, the phone rang and Kirsten picked it up.

'It's for you, Ryan,' she said. 'It's Trey.'

'Oh no!' thought Ryan. Trey was Ryan's brother. He was calling from prison. When Trey phoned, trouble always followed. Ryan took the phone outside.

'Hey, little brother,' Trey's voice sounded far away. 'Happy Thanksgiving.'

'You, too,' said Ryan. 'What do you want?'

'Can't I call my little brother to say hi?' said Trey. When Ryan didn't answer, he added, 'There is one thing ...'

'I knew there would be something,' thought Ryan.

'I wanted to ask you to come and see me,' said Trey.

'Oh, yes. OK,' said Ryan. Perhaps there wasn't going to be trouble after all. Perhaps Trey just wanted to see Ryan.

Ryan went back into the kitchen. 'Trey wants me to visit him,' he said. He felt pleased. Maybe this was a new start for the two of them. 'Um ... Could I borrow the car?'

'Yes, of course,' said Kirsten, giving him the keys. 'We'll have dinner when you get back.'

'Thanks,' said Ryan, smiling at Kirsten. The Cohens were very good to him.

He got into the car and turned the key. Then there was a knock on the window. He looked up to see Marissa standing there. He smiled and opened the window. She leaned in and gave him a kiss.

'What are you doing here?' he asked.

'I came to have dinner with my mom, but she isn't here,' said Marissa. 'Where are you going?'

'I'm going to see my brother.'

'Why don't I come with you?' Marissa said.

Ryan didn't want to say no. But he didn't want Marissa to see the prison.

'No, I don't think so. It's not a good idea,' he said.

'I'm coming,' she said, opening the car door and sitting down. 'It'll be fun.'

'It won't be fun,' said Ryan. 'Prison isn't fun.'

'I don't care,' said Marissa. 'I'm coming with you anyway.'

***

At the prison, Trey was waiting for Ryan. He wasn't really interested in seeing him – he had something for him to do.

'I want you to get my car from Arturo's house, and take it to Gattas's garage,' said Trey, as soon as Ryan got there.

Ryan didn't know what to say. Trey's car was stolen. He didn't want to do this.

'I'm busy today,' Ryan began. 'It's Thanksgiving and …'

'Busy? Busy eating turkey with your rich friends? I'm locked up here and you're too busy reading books and eating turkey?'

'OK,' said Ryan, feeling bad. 'I'll take the car for you. But nothing else. OK?'

'Thanks,' said Trey. 'You're a good brother, you know that?'

But Ryan felt nervous. He'd never met Gattas before.

***

Ryan and Marissa drove together to Chino. Ryan was quiet and Marissa understood why. This was a different world to Newport. The streets were dirty and most of the houses looked poor. At last Ryan stopped outside a small, brightly painted house.

'Is this your old house?' Marissa asked.

'No, it's Arturo's – a friend of my brother's,' said Ryan. He knocked on the door.

The door opened and a very attractive dark-haired girl stood there. She was about the same age as Ryan and Marissa.

'Ryan!' she cried. She threw her arms around him. 'Where have you been for the last five months?'

'Hey, Theresa,' Ryan said.

'Who's that?' asked the girl, looking at Marissa.

'This is Marissa,' said Ryan.

'Is she your new girlfriend?'

'Well ...' began Ryan, and suddenly Marissa understood.

'Oh …' she said, 'you two …'

'Yes,' said Theresa. 'I was the girl next door. You'd better come in.'

Marissa followed Theresa into the kitchen. She was preparing the Thanksgiving dinner.

'I'm going to get the car,' Ryan said and left the girls together. Marissa watched Theresa washing potatoes.

'Can I help?' she asked.

'No, it's OK,' said Theresa. 'You don't want to get your hands dirty.'

Marissa hated Theresa already. She was sexy and confident. And tough. Marissa could understand why Ryan had liked her.

'Hey,' said Ryan, coming back, 'I've got to take this car over to the garage now. Marissa can stay with you, can't she, Theresa?' he said.

'You're not leaving me here,' Marissa said quickly. 'I'm coming with you.'

Theresa stared at her and Marissa felt bad. But she didn't want to stay in the kitchen with Ryan's old girlfriend.

'You can't come with me,' Ryan said. 'It isn't safe. If you don't want to wait here, you can take Kirsten's car. I'll find a way home.'

'OK,' said Marissa.

She went out to Kirsten's car and got in. She looked in the mirror and watched Ryan. He was standing next to Theresa. Marissa felt jealous. Was Ryan going back to his old life? But there was nothing she could do. She started the engine and drove away.

Ryan did not want to go back to his old life. Chino didn't feel like home now, and although he still really liked Theresa, she was a part of Chino. But Ryan wanted to tell Theresa how bad he felt. Bad for leaving her all those months ago. Bad for leaving without saying goodbye. He couldn't find the words.

'See you then,' he said.

Theresa was not sure if Ryan was ever coming back. 'Good luck,' she said.

'You, too,' said Ryan. 'And … you know. Sorry.'

Theresa ran back into the house, the tears falling freely now.

CHAPTER 7
Thanksgiving

Ryan drove into Gattas's garage. There were a lot of tough guys working there. 'So these guys don't take holidays,' thought Ryan.

Gattas opened the car door. 'Are you Ryan?'

'Yes, here's the car,' said Ryan, and he threw the keys to Gattas and turned to walk away.

But Gattas hadn't finished with him yet. 'I've been waiting for this car for six months!' he said. 'There's some interest to pay.'

'I … haven't got any money,' said Ryan nervously. The other men had stopped working.

'Well, you're not just walking away,' said Gattas, and he stood in front of Ryan and hit him hard in the face.

Blood poured out of Ryan's nose. Ryan was terrified. He was alone. There was no escape. Gattas's friends were moving closer to him and they didn't look friendly.

Suddenly, Ryan heard a car drive fast into the garage. The men jumped out of the way. Gattas looked round and Ryan hit him as quickly as he could.

'Get in!' shouted Marissa. Before Ryan could even shut the door behind him, Marissa was driving away from Chino as fast as she could.

***

'Are you OK?' she asked him.

'Yeah,' he said. 'But what were you doing at Gattas's garage?'

'I followed you,' she said.

'You followed me?' Ryan thought about that for a

minute. 'Good idea,' he said, finally.

He looked at Marissa and realised he was in love with her. Only he wasn't ready to tell her – not yet. He just sat next to her and let her drive.

'There's one more visit to make,' he said.

***

'Right,' said Ryan to Trey. 'I took the car to Gattas. The trouble's over between you two. But I'm never doing anything for you again. Understand?'

Trey looked over at Marissa, waiting for Ryan. 'Yes,' he said, 'I understand.'

***

Back in Newport, Seth was having the best Thanksgiving of his life! Anna had come for dinner with his family. She was talking to his parents and they really liked her.

There was a knock at the door. It was Summer!

'What are you doing here?' he asked.

'I'm trying to have Thanksgiving with Marissa at her mom's house,' said Summer. 'But she's not there. And … I wanted to talk to you about what happened on the yacht.'

Seth was confused. He didn't want Anna to see Summer. She might feel upset. But he didn't want to send Summer away.

Suddenly, he had an idea. 'We can talk in the pool house,' he said. 'Come round this way.'

Summer looked at Seth as if he was crazy, but she followed him anyway.

'Wait here,' he said. 'I'll be back in a minute,' and he ran back to Anna.

'Where have you been?' Anna asked him.

'Oh, I was … feeding the fish in the pool house.'
'You've got some fish? Can I come and see them?'
'No …' said Seth. 'They just died, I'm sorry. It's terrible. Look, why don't I show you my bedroom? Let's go upstairs.'

Anna looked round the room and then started kissing him. It was nice. Very nice. But Seth couldn't stop thinking of Summer in the pool house. 'I need a plan,' he thought. But this was getting too complicated!

'I just need to make a quick phone call,' he said to Anna.

He ran back downstairs and out to the pool house. He opened the door to the pool house and Summer pushed him onto the bed.

'This isn't really happening!' thought Seth.

'We shouldn't be doing this,' said Summer after a few minutes. 'Let's go and get something to eat.'

'No!' shouted Seth. 'You're the guest. I'll go. You stay here.'

'I'd better go and check Anna's OK,' he thought, and he ran back upstairs. Before he could think of a plan, Anna started kissing him again.

'I should check the potatoes,' he said after a couple of minutes.

But it was too late. He got to the bottom of the stairs and Summer walked in. He turned to see Anna coming down. Anna looked at Summer. Summer looked at Anna. They both looked at Seth, and then they both walked out of the house.

***

'What am I going to do?' Seth asked Sandy.

'Just tell them the truth,' said Sandy, laughing. But what was the truth? Seth liked Anna – she was funny and clever and cute. And Seth liked Summer, because she was … Summer. He didn't want to lose either of them. It was impossible.

'Is this really happening to me?' he thought happily.

CHAPTER 8
Christmas shopping

'I'd like to introduce you to something I call … Chrismukkah,' said Seth one morning. Just then the front door opened and Sandy appeared, carrying a huge Christmas tree. Ryan hurried across the room to help him.

'Chrismukkah,' Seth continued, 'is the best of both worlds – the best of Christmas and the best of Hanukkah.*'

'Here,' he said, giving something to Ryan.

'I thought we agreed – no gifts,' said Ryan.

'This is different.'

Ryan looked at the gift. It was a red stocking with RYAN written on it.

'We all have one,' said Seth.

Ryan didn't say anything. He didn't want to be ungrateful, but he didn't want a stocking.

'How did you celebrate Christmas at home?' Sandy asked Ryan. 'If there's anything you'd like to do, tell us.'

Ryan was quiet. He thought about Christmas back in Chino. His mom used to get really drunk and forget to buy food.

---

* Seth's father is from a Jewish family and celebrates the winter holiday of Hanukkah.

'You can hang up the stocking if you want,' said Seth, feeling bad for his friend.

'Maybe later. I've got some work to do,' said Ryan. He really didn't want to think about Christmas, and he walked out to the pool house.

***

Ryan had no money to buy gifts, but he wanted to get the Cohens something to show how grateful he was. Maybe Marissa could help him find the right present. So that Saturday, Ryan and Marissa went Christmas shopping.

Neiman Marcus was the biggest, most expensive department store in the shopping centre. It was all lit up for Christmas.

'Do people really buy these things?' asked Ryan. He picked up a dog bowl that cost 250 dollars.

But Marissa was enjoying herself. She was trying on some make-up.

'I like it here. Everything's so perfect. You buy the right pair of shoes and all your problems fly away!' she said.

She picked up a very expensive watch and turned it over in her hand. 'But Dad doesn't give me money for shopping anymore.'

'Come on,' said Ryan. He didn't want Marissa to get sad. 'Let's go somewhere less expensive.'

They went back to the car park.

Marissa was opening the car door when a security guard hurried towards them.

'Excuse me,' he said. 'I'm going to have to check your bag.'

'What?' said Marissa.

'You've made a mistake,' started Ryan.

'Give me your bag, please, or I'll have to call the police,' the security guard repeated.

Marissa looked at Ryan. Then she slowly gave the guard her bag. Her hands were shaking.

The guard emptied the bag. Ryan's eyes opened wide when he saw the new make-up and the expensive watch that she had been looking at. Ryan stared at her.

'What have you been doing?' he asked, but Marissa couldn't speak. She dropped her head and started to cry.

***

Seth was waiting for Ryan in the pool house. Ryan came in, looking even more fed up than he had in the morning.

'How was shopping?' asked Seth.

'Strange.'

'Strange! So now I know everything about it!' laughed Seth.

'Sorry,' said Ryan. He realised he was being unfriendly to Seth because he felt unhappy. But it wasn't Seth's fault.

'I went to Neiman Marcus with Marissa and she … took some things.'

'Took some things? You mean she was stealing?'

'Yeah,' said Ryan.

'Wow,' said Seth, 'that is strange. I guess Marissa is having a really bad time at home.'

'Yes, I know,' said Ryan. 'But I don't know how I can help her.'

'Well, she'll be at the Newport Group party tonight,' said Seth, throwing Ryan a tie. 'Sounds like you'd better be there too.'

***

Marissa was sitting in the furthest corner of the security guard's office. She didn't want to be there. The guard had called her dad. It seemed like hours before Jimmy got there. When the door finally opened, Marissa jumped up and ran to him. But then she stopped. Julie was standing behind Jimmy.

'Why did you ask *her* to come?' Marissa cried.

'That's enough,' said Julie. 'My Marissa stealing? My Marissa a criminal? What's the matter with you?'

'Let's stay calm,' said Jimmy, but then Julie turned to him.

'So you're going to forgive her, are you? Well, we know who taught her to steal …'

'Stop it!' said Marissa, feeling even worse now her parents were fighting again. 'This is my fault, not Dad's.'

'Yes, well, you can tell the therapist all about it,' said Julie and Marissa stared at her.

'Mom, no! I'm not talking to a therapist. I'm not crazy. Dad, tell her!'

'It might help,' said Jimmy. 'Talk to someone about why you are doing things like this. Then things will get better.'

'Things will get better if she leaves me alone,' said Marissa.

Julie pretended not to hear. 'We have a party to get ready for …' she said.

'You're not expecting me to go to the Newport Group party?' said Marissa quietly.

'Yes, I am,' said Julie. 'No one there knows anything. Listen, Marissa, I love you. I am just trying to help …'

'Whatever,' said Marissa suddenly. 'Hey, we should go – Mom needs to get back to Caleb.' She walked quickly out of the room, leaving her parents to follow.

CHAPTER 9
Chrismukkah

Thousands of white lights were hanging from the trees outside the Newport Group offices. As Seth arrived with his parents, he smiled to himself. He loved Christmas. He picked up a plate and went straight to the cake table. Anna, dressed all in red, was waiting for him.

'Mistletoe!' she said brightly.

Seth smiled and leaned forward to kiss her.

'You look great,' he said. 'Wait there – I'll get some drinks.'

Seth headed for the bar, but before he got there, Summer stopped him.

'Hi,' she said holding mistletoe over him. She kissed him and Seth kissed her back, but he knew Anna was watching.

Seth realised the party could be difficult. He really needed Ryan to give him advice. He wanted to be friends with Summer *and* Anna, but they both seemed to want … more. He started looking for Ryan, but instead he found Anna who pulled him into an empty room.

'I've got a present for you,' she said.

It was a comic book she had made herself.

'*The Amazing Adventures of Seth Cohen*,' read Seth. 'You made me this? About me?'

'So do you like it?'

'Like it? I love it! It's the best present I've ever had,' he said, kissing her. A comic book? Anna had to be the girl for him. He led her back to the party. They were both smiling.

'Want to come and meet my dad?' she asked, but Seth shook his head.

'Later, OK? I need to find Ryan.' Seth wanted to check that Ryan was OK.

But Seth didn't find Ryan. He found Summer.

'Cohen, follow me,' said Summer. Seth couldn't stop himself. Moments ago he had been sure that Anna was the right girl for him. But he couldn't even speak when Summer was near. She pulled him into a different room.

'You like comic books, don't you?'

'Yeah …'

'Merry Christmas!' she said.

Summer let her dress fall to the floor. Under it she was dressed as Wonder Woman*.

Seth did not know what to do next.

'I should get a drink …' he said.

'You're not going anywhere,' said Summer, pulling Seth to her. 'What's that?'

She had noticed the comic book.

* Wonder Woman was a star in one of the first ever comic books.

'Oh, Anna made it. For Christmas.'

'She made this?' Summer started looking through it. 'It's amazing,' she said quietly. She felt stupid now, dressed as Wonder Woman.

Then the door opened and Anna came in.

'Seth? Are you there?' she called, then stopped as she saw him with Summer.

'Hey, Anna,' said Seth going red in the face. 'Summer was just giving me my Christmas present.'

'Oh my God,' said Anna staring at Summer. 'You're Wonder Woman and I made Seth a comic book? How old am I? Eight?'

'No, Anna, wait ...' Seth said, but she was already moving towards the door.

'You should stay,' Summer said, putting her dress back on. 'I'll go. I'm sorry.'

'It's not your fault,' said Anna.

'You're right. It's not my fault and it's not your fault either ...'

They both looked at Seth.

'Ladies, please ...' started Seth.

Summer stopped him. 'Listen, I like you,' she said, 'but so does she. And if you don't choose ...'

'... someone's going to get hurt,' finished Anna, and they both walked out of the room.

Seth watched them go. He didn't want to choose. Why couldn't they all be friends?

***

Marissa didn't feel brave enough to talk to anyone. She stood near an upstairs window where she could drink from a bottle of Scotch* without being seen. She'd taken it

* Scotch whisky.

from her dad's. If she had to see a therapist anyway, she didn't need to worry how much she drank.

When Ryan finally arrived, she ran downstairs and threw her arms around him.

'There you are! Did you miss me?' she asked.

'You OK?' he asked uncertainly.

'I am now that you're here,' she said, pulling his shirt.

Ryan pulled away. 'Had a few drinks?' he asked.

'Want to catch up?' Marissa said, waving the bottle at him.

'No,' Ryan said taking her arm. 'We're getting out of here.'

'Oh,' sighed Marissa. 'I'm only having fun.'

'That's what my mom used to say,' said Ryan. 'What are

you doing?'

Marissa was getting out her car keys and walking towards her car.

'You can't drive!' shouted Ryan.

'Shut up!' cried Marissa and climbed into the front seat of her car. Ryan ran to stop her, but she locked the doors. Ryan watched helplessly as she backed the car into a wall. A light broke. She stopped the car and started crying.

'Open the doors,' said Ryan. 'I'll drive.'

He drove away from the party, taking the coast road. Marissa took the bottle out of her bag and opened it.

'Stop it!' said Ryan.

'Why? I'm not driving.'

'No, because you've already had too much.'

'I haven't.'

'Oh no!' said Ryan. 'I don't believe it!' There was a police car behind them.

Ryan stopped the car and Marissa hid the bottle under her skirt.

The policeman asked for Ryan's papers. 'You've got a broken back light,' he said.

'It just happened,' said Ryan. 'We're taking the car to a garage.'

'Have you kids been drinking?' he asked.

'No' said Ryan, and Marissa shook her head.

'You get to a garage, OK?' said the policeman. 'Happy holidays!'

Ryan stayed in the car, watching the policeman drive away. Then he walked round to Marissa's side and opened the door. He took the bottle of Scotch and threw it as far as he could. Then he slammed the door shut. Opened it and slammed it ... again and again.

'Stop it!' cried Marissa. 'You're frightening me!'

'Good!' Ryan shouted. 'Because you're frightening me.' He slammed the door a final time then got back in the driver's seat.

'If there's drinking, crying and policemen … then I guess it's Christmas,' he said, calmer now. 'I left all these problems in Chino. I'm not doing it again.'

Marissa understood what he was saying. 'OK,' she said quietly.

***

The next morning, Seth and Ryan were having breakfast in silence. They were both thinking about the night before.

'I have no idea what to do,' Seth said, staring into his coffee.

'You're asking the wrong guy,' replied Ryan.

Sandy came downstairs looking for coffee.

'Hey, guys, what's the matter?' he said.

'Don't ask,' said Seth.

'Marissa and I had a fight,' said Ryan.

'Sorry to hear that,' said Sandy. 'Listen, you two, it's the holidays. Maybe we should all go and see a movie …'

'I have to see Marissa today,' said Ryan. 'She's going to see a therapist and I told her I'd go with her.'

'You could,' Sandy said, sitting down next to him, 'but you don't have to.'

'What do you mean?'

'She's been having a hard time, hasn't she?' said Sandy. 'But Marissa has parents. And you have us. You don't need to look after everyone anymore. You could have some fun.'

Ryan thought about it. Perhaps Sandy was right. Perhaps Marissa needed some time too.

Ryan got up and headed to the living room. Seth and Sandy followed him. What was he going to do next? He picked up his stocking and hung it up over the fire, next to Seth's. Then Ryan turned to look at his friends.

'Happy Christmas, guys,' he said and smiled.

FACT FILE

The coolest job

They mix with the stars, they wear great clothes and they get paid for it all! But what do the actors really think about working on The OC? Is it really as cool as it sounds? And how did they get the job in the first place?

On ... getting the part

Chris Carmack (Luke):
I didn't think I'd get the part because I'm nothing like Luke. But I knew lots of guys like Luke in high school.

Adam Brody (Seth):
I ad-libbed some of my lines. I wanted to give Seth Cohen a bit more personality. I think the producers liked what I did!

Rachel Bilson (Summer):
I was quite confident when I auditioned for The OC as I'd met girls like Summer. I was the first to read for the part and I got it! So that was cool.

Samaire Armstrong (Anna):
I couldn't believe it when I was asked to play Anna. But it feels right. We're very similar and we have the same taste in clothes!

On ... the other actors

Rachel Bilson (Summer):
We're all good friends. Mischa, Samaire and I talk about make-up and guys and fashion and it helps with our relationships in the show.

Melinda Clarke (Julie):
I grew up in the real OC so I know that way of life! I love spending time with Kelly Rowan (Kirsten Cohen) and the girls.

Peter Gallagher (Sandy):
I really like the kids. I learn as much from them as they do from me.

in the world?

On ... being famous

Ben McKenzie (Ryan):
I'm proud of the show and its success. I love living in California, but I'm from Texas and I miss the life there. I don't think I've changed as a person. Success doesn't change who you are.

Adam Brody (Seth):
I have to put my head down if we're walking past a group of girls or they go crazy! That feels weird. Sometimes I like to pretend I'm still a guy who nobody knows.

Mischa Barton (Marissa):
I live with my mum in a small apartment in LA while I'm filming. My dad and sister, Hania, live in New York and I get homesick sometimes.

Chris Carmack (Luke):
It's amazing to be part of something that is so popular. My family love *The OC* too. They say they'd like it even if I wasn't in it!

Would you like to work on a show like *The OC*? Why / Why not?

What do these words mean? You can use a dictionary.
part   ad-lib   audition   relationship   homesick   weird

FACT FILE

Adam Brody

Adam Brody plays Seth Cohen, the geek we all love to love. Adam grew up in San Diego, far from the designer parties of Newport Beach. But how similar is the actor to his TV character?

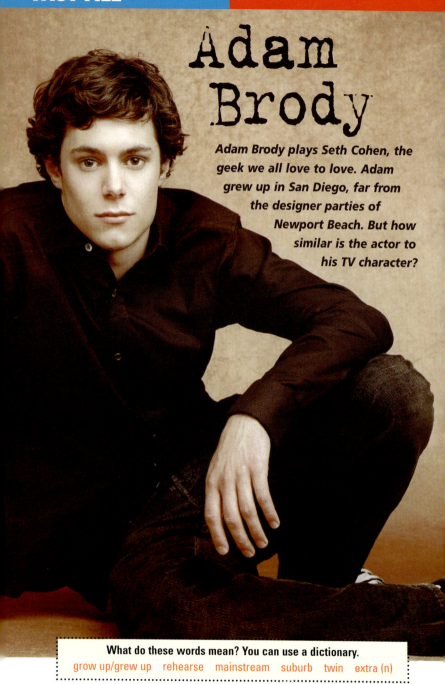

What do these words mean? You can use a dictionary.
grow up/grew up   rehearse   mainstream   suburb   twin   extra (n)

In what ways are you similar to Seth Cohen?

We wear the same type of clothes. Sometimes when we're rehearsing, people ask me if I'm dressed as Seth! Seth is not mainstream in his music tastes and neither am I. I listen to independent bands like *Death Cab for Cutie*.

How are you different?

I'm not very good with computers. I'm only just learning how to use the Internet! But Seth's a bit of a geek and he loves PlayStation. I didn't take my school studies very seriously. I was really into surfing and that was all I wanted to do. And I think I'm a bit more confident with girls than he is!

Do you know the real OC?

No, I grew up in San Diego. It was just an ordinary suburb – nothing like the OC – but it was a good place to grow up. Seth's an only child, but I've got twin younger brothers.

Seth Cohen is in love with both Summer and Anna. Who would you choose?

I like girls with cool styles of their own, like Anna. Summer spends too much time worrying about the latest designer clothes. And I hate seeing girls with little dogs in their handbags. A dog in a handbag isn't a dog in my opinion! But sometimes a girl can surprise you, when she isn't how she seems …

Have you always wanted to be an actor?

No, I had no idea what to do when I left school. A friend told me about being an extra. He had appeared in *Power Rangers*. I thought that was amazing! I got a job parking cars at Beverly Hills hotel and looked for work as an extra. Then one day I got a small speaking part. And that was how it all started!

What do you think of Seth Cohen? Is he cool or is he a geek?

FACT FILE

Under age? What

Wild parties. Big cars. It looks as if the kids on The OC can do what they want! But there are laws about what you can and can't do in America, as there are everywhere.

Drinking

How old? In the UK and most of Europe, you have to be 18 years old to drink in a bar. The US has one of the highest legal drinking ages in the world – you have to be 21 before you can buy an alcoholic drink.

The issue: Under age drinking. In the UK, under age drinking is a big problem. Teenagers may have private parties at home where they drink alcohol. Some people think that the legal drinking age in the UK should go up to 21 years old. Then teenagers who drink under age might be older, for example, 18 rather than 14. But in the US, many people believe that the drinking age should drop to 18 years. If this happened, perhaps there would be fewer private parties and young people would drink more sensibly in bars and clubs.

What do you think? How old should you be to buy alcohol? Is under age drinking a problem in your country?

What do these words mean? You can use a dictionary.

alcohol/alcoholic   under age   legal   consent   get divorced

the law says...

Getting married

How old? In the UK, you can get married at the age of 18, or 16 with a parent's consent. In Scotland, you can legally get married at 16 and you don't need your parents' agreement. Some young British couples run away to Scotland to get married.

In some countries, women can get married younger than men. For example, in China, men have to be 22, but women can be 20.

The issue: Divorce. Are teenage weddings a big mistake? Some people think so. Almost 50% of divorces in the US are between people who got married under the age of 18. However, only 24% of people who are married after the age of 25 get divorced.

What do you think? How old should you be to get married? Why do people get divorced, do you think?

Driving

How old? In the UK, you can learn to drive when you are 17. In the US, learning to drive takes time! In California, you can learn to drive when you are 15 – but only if there is someone over 25 in the car with you. But you can't take your driving test until you are 18. When you first pass your test, you are not allowed to drive at night or with a passenger in the car.

The issue: Safety. Teenage drivers have more accidents than older drivers. And British teenagers have more road accidents than American kids. Over 50% of teenage drivers in the UK talk on the phone or send text messages while they are driving.

What do you think? How old should you be to drive? Do younger drivers drive less carefully than older drivers?

SELF-STUDY ACTIVITIES

Chapters 1–3

Before you read

1. Match each word to its definition. You can use a dictionary.

   apartment   charity event   ferris wheel   jealous
   misfit   therapist   water polo

   a) a big wheel with seats on it
   b) a professional person who gives advice to people with problems
   c) feeling angry or unhappy because someone has something which you want
   d) someone who is very different from other people in a place
   e) a flat
   f) a party, match or show which is organised to collect money
   g) a ball game played by swimmers

2. Complete the sentences with the correct tense of the verbs. You can use a dictionary.

   break up   catch up   fit in   get divorced   sigh

   a) Alison was tired. 'This work is so boring,' she … .
   b) I was very ill in April and missed a lot of school. When I went back, I had a lot of … to do.
   c) In the UK, one in three married couples … .
   d) My cousin has … with his girlfriend – they had been together since university.
   e) The guys in my new class seem very different from me – I'm not sure if I'm going to … .

After you read

3. Are these sentences true or false? Correct the false sentences.

   a) Ryan spent the summer in Juvie.
   b) Marissa is living with her mom.
   c) Luke is still in love with Marissa.
   d) Seth Cohen is popular at Harbor School.
   e) Sandy Cohen is like a father to Ryan.
   f) Ryan finds the school work easy.
   g) Anna lives in Pittsburg.
   h) Summer and Seth are good friends.

4 What do you think?
  a) Will Seth become Anna's boyfriend?
  b) Will Ryan and Marissa become a couple?
  c) Will Ryan stay out of trouble?

Chapters 4–6

Before you read
  5 Choose the correct answer. You can use a dictionary.
   a) Which of these is another word for a boat with a sail?
   ship   truck   yacht
   b) Which of these means 'very surprised and upset'?
   nervous   proud   shocked
   c) Which of these means 'strong' but can also be used to describe a criminal?
   weak   tough   jealous
   d) Which of these are you doing if you look at someone for a long time?
   staring   sharing   shaking

After you read
  6 Complete the sentences with the correct name.
  Caleb   Jimmy   Kirsten   Summer   Theresa   Trey
   a) Caleb Nichol is …'s father.
   b) … is Julie's new boyfriend.
   c) Julie says she wants to get back together with … .
   d) … is jealous of Anna.
   e) … is Ryan's old girlfriend.
   f) Ryan's brother is called … .

  7 What do you think?
   a) Will Ryan go back to live in Chino?
   b) Will Ryan see Theresa again?
   c) Will Marissa's parents get back together?
   d) Will Seth choose Anna or Summer?

SELF-STUDY ACTIVITIES

Chapters 7–9

Before you read

8 Match each word to its definition. You can use a dictionary.
   mistletoe   security guard   slam   stocking
   a) shut a door with a loud noise
   b) a plant which has small white fruit at Christmas
   c) someone who stops people stealing from a shop
   d) a large sock which is filled with gifts at Christmas

9 Which of these celebrations are described below?
   carnival   Christmas   Hanukkah   Thanksgiving.
   a) a twelve day celebration in December
   b) an eight day Jewish holiday in December
   c) a party where there are rides and games and which is usually outside (US English)
   d) a public holiday in the US in November

After you read

10 Answer these questions.
   a) How does Marissa save Ryan from Gattas and his men?
   b) After taking the car back to the garage, what does Ryan tell Trey?
   c) What does Sandy suggest Seth tells Anna and Summer?
   d) At the department store, why does the security guard stop Marissa?
   e) Who do Jimmy and Julie suggest that Marissa talks to?
   f) At the Newport Group party, why do Anna and Summer hold mistletoe over Seth's head?
   g) Why do the police stop Marissa and Ryan?

11 Write words to describe …
   a) Anna   b) Summer   c) Seth   d) Marissa   e) Ryan

12 What do you think?
   a) Why does Marissa steal things from the department store?
   b) Why is Ryan so angry that Marissa is drinking Scotch?
   c) Will Ryan and Marissa stay together?
   d) Who in the book do you think is a misfit?